HAMMERTOWN

Hammertown

Peter Culley

 NEW STAR BOOKS | VANCOUVER | 2003

Some of the following poems were previously published in the book *The Climax Forest* and in *Public, The Capilano Review, Boo, Ecopoetics, Open City, Monkey Puzzle, Raddle Moon*, and *West Coast Line*. Thanks too to the persons and institutions that enabled me to give readings, and the audiences who listened.   — PC

Publication of this work is made possible by grants from the Canada Council, the British Columbia Arts Council, and the Department of Canadian Heritage Book Publishing Industry Development Program.

Printed and bound in Canada
First printing August 2003

New Star Books Ltd.
107 - 3477 Commercial Street
Vancouver, BC   V5N 4E8
www.NewStarBooks.com
info@NewStarBooks.com

NATIONAL LIBRARY OF CANADA CATALOGUING IN PUBLICATION DATA

Culley, Peter, 1958–
  Hammertown / Peter Culley.

  Poems.
  ISBN 1-55420-000-8

  1. Nanaimo (B.C.) — Poetry. I. Title.
PS8555.U48H35 2003   C811'.54   C2003–911111–3

Greetings from Hammertown   1

The Provisions   6

A Winter Visitation   9

Paris 1919   12

The Book of Hugh   15

The Iron Mountains   19

Snake Eyes

    A Poem for the English Poets   23

    A Book of Quiet Numbers   29

    Woodland Suite   35

    Homage to Quiz   44

    Dedicated to You But You Weren't Listening   47

    Reasons Why I Mumble   51

House Is a Feeling   59

The Voice of Kathy Sledge   63

A Letter from Hammertown
   to East Vancouver and the East Village   66

Eight Views of Ornamental Avenue   70

Journey to the West   80

Morse's Code   83

Once — and this is something he had never done for anyone and would never do again — he showed her the puzzle he was reassembling that fortnight: it was a fishing port on Vancouver Island, a place called Hammertown, all white with snow, with a few low houses and some fishermen in fur-lined jackets hauling a long, pale hull along the shore.

GEORGES PEREC
Life A User's Manual

In *front* of the wall, a sort of scrimmage is taking place — arms, discs, etc., the abstract forces are trying to pile themselves up into a permanent mound — BUT — a hammer looming in from the top-side is definitely hitting this structure, making it seem as if it is crumbling, collapsing.

PHILIP GUSTON

Greetings from Hammertown

Huge uproar lords it wide.
A tim'rous grader halts
before an overflowing ditch, its
big bad boy body slumped
as if thwarted at its gigging.
In the shed's cartoon shadow
wee dinosaurs sport and romp, their urgent
    territorial beefs
strangely comforting somehow.
The missives of October
    tonk against the upstairs windows
like desperate and ancient flies . . .

. . . fuck 'em.
I tried to climb the glass mountain
    but I kept hitting
the glass ceiling, so
If you want to read
    "decay"
into this rocky heap
of nasty moss, this
eggy newspaper intrusion, that's your
    quattrocento prerogativo —
but the pheasant remains,
nailed to the outhouse door, the hare
    limps trembling past the dozin' cat, the sedges
and streams of my late youth
    cleared and flattened for you
even as I write this;
the damp air does not retard enlightenment,
the engine of progress rests upon granite blocks.

Close crowds the shining atmosphere, luminous
smoke billows orange
from the banked woodfires
of the working class, where earlier
a row of beets had bloomed
        into a gleaming wound
beneath the suddenly open sky

        Alas, the streets of Hammertown
are certainly strange,
the few who walk them
hunched in the posture of exile,
past grim houses with curtains
drawn tight
against the encroaching
and inky night,
        . . . past
the park's leaf-stuffed
artillery
which points toward
the empty middle distance
beyond the boarded laundromat, as
do the birdshit-streaked copper eyes
of the founding father, whose massive hands
rest blankly upon the open pages
of a blank and massive copper book.

Alas, in Hammertown
        the days move like bugs
or slugs, leaving translucent trails.
The days move like horned snails.
Mountains, fields and forests
move through my brain
in a flood
of light
controlled by blood,

until, coming into focus
the torn memory of another —
I don't know why I bother.
Seated on an autumn boulder
dappled sandstone
above my shoulder,
a neat cube
of green light
(if I'm not mistaken)
was where I took
the seat not taken.
Across the concourse
my double, of course, was
a book of matches
idly with involved:
he would not meet my gaze
nor I his,
he lives in my house
    and is writing this . . .

Below the unsightly plain
a brown deluge, near that edge
that is a zone
of permanent permission, where
the damp exhausted firework of *polis*
bobs to the surface of a tainted puddle,
    where cattle from untasted fields do
    bitterly return, their lowing ting'd
    with unhealthy intelligence, that
light industrial
lunapark, where those that take
their pastime in the troubled air
gather in knots
of intransigence
and woe
pouring their curses into

the dark flow.
Struggling through
a dissipated grove
one comes at last
to a version of a path —
thus delineated
there is no room
for hesitation—
　　　but it is all hesitation—
the woodpecker
rears back
and slams
its full weight, all the power
In its teeny shoulders—
　　　PECK!
Into the unyielding spruce—
　　　PECK!
PECK!
　　　PECK!
and works it right out
and slams it right out
and clears it right out
　　　and erases the blackboard
　　　and erases the tape
　　　and pops the lid off
　　　and tears the roof off
　　　and boils it right down
from an oil tanker
to a teaspoon.

At length, into the obscure
forest came the vision
I had sought
through grief and shame —
a caravan
of bright yellow trucks,

jostling like bland-mugged thugs
along a granulate roadway
of broken bottles, bristling
with crab claws, with arms like
monstrous barbed
dog cocks, depositing
layer after layer of
sulphurous spoor
into a vale of rubber smoke.

    Sleep frighted flies,
    and round the rocking dome
    howls the savage blast . . .

The Provisions

Between the cannon
    and the father,
between the thicket
    and the cave of light
a large rectangle
of lawn, deeply scored
with muddy tracks, a scattering
of minor trash, loaded
and sodden as is customary
for such places, drainage mostly
a matter of chance —
    an impromptu canal
formed by loose shoes and bike
gouges over the course
of a winter, emptying into
a vast depression
in the roadway —
such matters convened
under the heading
    "infrastructure"
are a species
of art, that is
attended to
sporadically
by hooded figures
walking on their knees
down endless halls
    of polished granite.

Odd patterns
and congruences
of traffic, birdflight, roofing
material, the high keening

wire, the thick pink
translucence
around the treetops; these
    are the maps, and
at that leafless edge
a cone of crosshatching wind
escapes from the mouth
of a little fat cloud.

    I named it
but I did not nail it —
from an ancient thicket
of blackberry
Leviathan emerges
with a bloody nose, lighting
his way with sparks
struck from the buckles
of his coat,
continues down
a street called Pine
that conduits
and is a spine
that wanders through, then
follows down
the underside
    of Hammertown
And skirts the rim
    as round a bowl
Of zoning slipped beyond control,
    then sudden low it passes wide
    a place that is all underside.
    Coming at last
to the park, enraged
    from the copper book
he tears a page . . .

Between the storms of October
and the storms of March
the deep, wide trench
of this afternoon, one
in a series making up
this temporal lapse, this
interregnum
in which we are involved —
ignorant as I am
I hardly dare to speak of it —
but the fabric of its projection
tears against
all the provisions
I can bring to bear —
the distant groaning metal
of non-being, the self
    afloat in a saucepan
    of burning sugar, myriads
    of little salts, shaped like
    double wedges
diffused through water
earth and æther.
A flock of what
resonates through the low thatch.
Retrieve the sample
as a dog would, its noble and stolid
shoulders versus
the booming cataract,
    because it knows nothing else,
    because I know nothing else.

A Winter Visitation

for Deanna Ferguson

    Little
hints of wildness
south of town, where the names
become numerals and then
again, where
tracts cinderblock rise from
bogs tumescent, and from them
      vast showrooms of icy light, which
         sear and tint th'
o'er-hanging clouds — perhaps a bear
      occasionally pads
through the low wood, upon
its shoulders a trumpeting
Mozartean infant, perhaps
a starveling deer, coaxed
from the hills
by sad necessity
gnaws the sugar canes
abandoned; or
whatever
      the cats drag in, little
      faces detached
      with epicurean disdain,
gazing blankward up
from the doormat.

Or north, where the numinous
avenues are bisected
by their names, where
tummocks rise above the plains
as if foreshortened
for engraving, as if indexed

9

in perspective's workbook — all of this
until that eve
unclear to me
(For I do not drive
    you see —)
and as a youth
I scarce required
sleight or misdiscretion
to find myself thus,
    utterly lost —
    by covering tight
    my ears and eyes, pressing
    into the cracked and cool
    leatherette of the
    armrest until
the boxy slab of darkness
    (that then I for the
void mistook)
rose inkily and warmly within,
So that registering through
the rear window
the bubble of the
voluptuously careening night
I was nowhere, nowhere, nowhere
    at last . . .

But here,
tombed rigid upfront, dusk
engorged upon
the shuttered fruitstand casts
pinky rectangles
steel poles wedged
in concrete cones welded
to the rocky undersurface
upon which the truck
the tracts, the stand

and all of the town
uneasy rests, fixed in turn
to that wobbling pivot
which twists and twitches 'gainst
the continental plate
    like a hallucinating adolescent . . .

Perhaps an owl
some hours hence
will hunting glide
above the golf course's
untainted snow, encircling
eastwards rising
by successive currents
will backwards scan
this recumbent skeleton of light —

    tapering by slow degree
    the northern halogen
    gives way to the orange argon
    of the south, defining
    as points upon a grid
    the set of broken teacups, humpy
    hillocks and scattered inscriptions
    of the sleeping world.

Paris 1919

for Kurt Cobain

I'd walk six miles
    out of my way
To hear again
    the slow decay
Of that piano,
    far away —

King Tubby's
    Studio A.

If it's a record the fade is replaced
    by the needle on the vinyl, its dusts and abrasions;
On certain old LPs
    pre-echo of the next

Cut? On CD analog tape hiss, studio bloom or

digital nothing —
    (a pressing upon the drum) —
    . . . as for the crickets in the wall, Sam Phillips
or Marshall Chess ordering coffee in the next room

I'm sure it's there —

I just can't hear it, not as

The pulpy sulphur rain is heard
    smelly falling
On Hammertown
    as it does on Aberdeen —
    (a long day out of doors not a possibility —)
    white bags of silage from upper window

glimpsed heaped
        against a black fence, the silence

Between tracks now filled with
        the highway's subcutaneous roar —
                and then Bo Diddley begins again, boxy guitar
        benign threatening
                across boxy hips, Jerome Green's massed
                        mercury groin spreading maracas —
        the fucked-up world
                pendant upon its rusty hinge
        works up refuelled
                for another spin . . .

As against it Young Werther,
        leaping from the roof of dad's garage
                is caught by verge soft
                        unseen hitherto, as day
                        upon day did day succeed, as pearly gray
                        against jack pine the day it silhouetted

Time, its demand and circumference, its cloth
        against the forehead dark,

Wanting vista
        Wanting space, a bit of prospect bold and breezy;
                a silence you could drive a truck through —
                        until someone did, and Parsifal was
                                out of brown
Paradise cast . . .

                Misty wallpaper roses,
                faces, light's tenses, hi-hat's
                scan of plaster grapes
                moulding, left to right and

      up a little —
       — screwy drifts dust
        bass spreading ranged
   from deep centre, should choose a
   harp and carpet, a cat to slip
   and steady, a rickety porch
   deserted, a mouse's
   mortgage, gargoyle earring
   demanding waving, narrow board crosses
   creosoted little thicket, light
   emitting manger, in April . . .

against the rocks
    the ranting, phallic
       nothing, the whirling

nowhere —
    out of the wooferless parched forest
       and onto the luminist seashore
(Brian Wilson *ca.* 1965)

    — a mix without edge or limit,
    monophonic and monocular, a continent
    buoyed by floating magnets
    beneath Saskatchewan.

The Book of Hugh

falls open
upon a bituminous and flaky
page of coal. In turning
from it lit upon
a pink and stripey rock
found early in the walk
a rejected tumbled pebble
that had through the air
appeared polished. Therefore
in a premature spring — the Christmas
greens still up — the toads
took to the roads, driven
by unseasonal lust
through the marsh gas
and into our path.

    The dim stir
of chemical atoms
toward an axis of crystal form:
thus bear spoor, formerly loose
and fruity becomes
parchment, chimneysmoke appears
to hover, the distant shunting
gravel is through the
drizzle oddly amplified.
Likewise the trance-like
life of plants: as for
the fern summer
so, roughly
winter — a fructose haze
foreboding not ever
a tender reading
that does not waver.

Beside us on the lawn
a brown barette
flecked with gold,
the photo of a horse,
in my hand
a pebble of no note, that had
gleamed in the mind only,
as upon the tracks
a red cent flattened oval
spun against the cutbank
and away.

   The ragged wall
of social habit
connecting boulders, half-
obliterated, etched over
aggregate a glyph-like
trace of hooves
out of the quarry
the gravel truck's
girlish sway upon the little curve.
From spray to spray
flitting light
the speckled finch's
yellow note above
the tufted and ossianic ridge
sepia splash along a margin
interior foxed, off white
endpaper snow
falling closing, scything
crow tinges blue
the green day's
republican starlings, sneering
ducks, fatuous
shitting geese . . .

Personality
an unseasonal squall, a "gesture"
(as in painting *ca.* 198–) —
a runny mustard splat, a pig's
black tail, a little silver
hurricane, an omni-browed
Kali — though
sleeve notes tell
a different story: puppyish
prospects considered
beneath sugary eastern elms,
exalted sleep, smeared mountains beyond
the desk, foreground's
heap of sulphur bestrides
the bridge's sexy parabola,
grainy against an edge
that is no edge
at all. Would seek therefore
a motive for its use, would
attempt unbidden
a tunnel
through the thick mantle
between us, the branch's
shadow on the shade moves
and is a bird
or isn't — too big
for a leaf certainly, though
similarly launched; inattention
fluid also, subject to
accumulation, massed
hesitations, blanks,
aphasic interludes.

Thus brick by brick
the pyramid of stupidity
is erected, so mortarless

suburban walls, the blue screen
of a false spring. Beaten
back incrementally
the peeping snowdrops
re-gather, rime's
erect buzz cut
atop a minor green shelf
of shale, omitted rain
yet fills the valley's
moist hollows, unseen
ripples athwart
the spongy ground.

The Iron Mountains

They glide
on thin ice
through stands
of crystallized birch
beside red farmhouses
ring'd with red rocks;
the iron mountains
mauve and impenetrable
in the horizonless distance —
a lean-to
fragile as a nest
straddles a
length of wire.
In the eerie half-light
of Haparanda
the buildings
on the opposite bank
resist definition,
oscillating
in and out of focus
as a sharp breeze
rises off the river.

They skate
who fall so easily
into the deep grey kingdom
of sleep, and dream
an idiot's dream
of order, a bridge
festooned with lights
odd and jagged
connecting each to each
across a fearful void —

and wake then
with a start, then
the carriage dark and empty
the nameless city
shattered somehow
into jagged and icy
shards of light, spinning
and careening
into the darkness.

Snake Eyes

A POEM FOR THE ENGLISH POETS

excoriate forks deform

the yellow wallflower stained

with iron forms cushioned

usage chloroforms the

evenings poplars theses en-

tomb the sleeping bee a plume

of purple methodist dust

well sir I am that quickly

stranded shandean if

in reply the shellacked wit-

ness on red table resists

stout work on fader toggle

sorted as for poppys dads

the word sleepy theory trim

dancehall chronometer grunts

chaplet dropout waverley

parish of light folds dewy

disco biscuit easement fluffs

out of linen dawn encrusts

ears thicket chorus of bursts

cranky bank of mid-range chill

maybe a little bud in

the modality tapped the

mountain dew where tasty chaos

blunts the april hay intakes

downdrafting finch citation

shears diminished fifths against

tristanos decrescendo

stills will staggers mauve gloam

straw poke with pea-green ribbons

through a screen of chilly's dots

a fine shag flock ornamented

with a light frieze equal to

the conduct of an empire

the management of a space

are flints moss of many sorts
flakes of gold clift in passing
out of the grotto and in-
to the wilderness soul shack
supported upon rustic
ameliorations soft
subject domain enclosure

foam-rot hudibrastics swell
daisy mitt bloat inky afters
clear spotting sediments mix
a short pour with a long wait
hot thistle joint core maps sheets of
down clusters of stutter monk
like dandelion time outs

milky bar shingle entails

scored with prints of precious hands

two-tone fiesta leaf drive

siskin swing felt plate versioned

chromatic sunbeam dub glints

across the old red sandstone

love shadows the old baby

jack your warehouse impairment

one fingers the rikers bus

tumescent mushtown bubba

prods the airshaft with lavender

steam bandaged tubby thumb

whorls against the wainscotings

bright ionic afterthought

the name of the thing one sees

is taxidermy vice

is a tower built upon

chicken pimpin habit slacks

rollbar crank economy

detailing wipes out old dutch

yeller laburnum shudder

sorry i dropped the wheeler

but not the needle damage

needs a cartridge a clockwise

tendency hat is not a

roof the bear in the barney

resists a cleansing cuddle

nuremburg love bites pop up

among the smug lawns pad great

cats ravels splayfoot blues tapped

essentialist alhambras

lino poodle click demo vibes

in pencil i dwell in stock

corvo inking fantasia

like poperys big green fist

an excess of tiny felt

poverty of iron hedged

the dour screens of preferment

against mays april the sixties

twenties astringent pastel

metrocolour lawnsmear grids

adumbrate years of rupert

to the inside of a curve

with no chance of error dread

pastoralists re-locate

bloater aesthetics firmly

within a kind of pink-cheeked

workplace rosicrucianism

tender as floating dickweed

a curiosly crena-

ted golfball lying in a

rousseauesque roughs kevins book

still stained remaindered with

seventies coffee unread-

able man of feeling in

tight suit mortgages montaigne

A BOOK OF QUIET NUMBERS

a book of quiet numbers

lies pretty pradaesque scrims

draping umber tone forests

o'er broiling seas of slippage

calcine spotted limewasher

cloudbanks crowd thatched margins

gray reread the shaded shed

honours too as well as gout

descend ferment and over-

flow hiss bibliographic

wax speech blue porch spackle

tossers glint on swivel gun

fix the gnocchi aurora

reglue the summers spoilers

suave civvy street gorillas

freeze with coos bark dazzle eye

contacts split with menaces

dandy phantom shoofly cola

sweats alpha sugar dustcoats

can calendar specked through

elapse yield thus to tams trig

no i wouldnt want to be

a kid about it

not if it meant heaping up

the days like then i did like

cottonballs on a shelf of

plexi cement plugs gainst

forlorn outbuildings nosing

it hangs its sheets in june
dismantles the island of
sleep in crisp suspensions dam-
eronian it hinges thirdstream
residue cabinessence
starched cool breeze hospital fold
refreshed palm a workbook warm

the flight deck flowers faded
into nuanced englished waves of
spurious feel re: the
rivers invite the cruisers
creek a charmless armoured fish-
faced man a damp mans damp hand
boiler beach bruce county ont.

high dessicate clouds fine winds
off-white smudge noreaster
smoke does not equal sign dis-
tressed lines three stacked anvil close
and play quote hammerhead thought
too tart for hard-wired humbo
too red sweet for wee soft beaks

groat woodbug swerving cata-
mount skint as pudding cool shelf
workshy parings drop jitter
kits too broke for fleer at the
hegemonic surrender
depot or tattoo on it
shelbys pound puppy dragster

intentions blizzard the hat
brims crisp waffle of snow for
whom who keeps a record the
birds uneasy roost the cats
grinning gritty dotage wuk
wuk the roaring traffics boom
boom in someone elses room

once bright moon precluded sleep

swarded materials neath

the sprinklers twitching arc shags

torpid emerald noondays

yield to needs blue scattering

evenings macaronic sled

smoky crackles blunt my trotters

a mouse a monster a men-

tal event placed its sculpted

thumb on the wet drapery

may rain and did rain

mysterious barricades

falling as in fragonards

wee pink skirting board jihads

starting from its silken couch

amassed the dooryards breezes

mealy-mouthed retainers tossed

with lateral rigour the

engine begins to totter

smoke correct and then describe

its infantile procedure

drier layter an offer

fielded hips and haws rent

the rosy prospects western

coronal flushed mezzotint

as was the a.m. that is

as always adjectival

repletion no death as such

WOODLAND SUITE

> *'the apple on its bough is her desire'*
> HART CRANE

> *'hometowns are reformist IDIOTS'*
> KEVIN DAVIES

woodland is the real kingsway

ginger the starling propane

huffer ingests at sunset

carved ivory pastilles flanked

alley ivy-bedecked deck

copper tailing rollo cough

scarless pastimes pierce nightbloom

discussions yeah but they still

went ahead and vetoed the

plan fair acushnet only

you are the climate girly

palm like palm glowing watchbird

ticking over benefit

triage of blue wheel smoke blue

creations rebels little

finches in big corn tone rows

farmers harmonicas sucked

by octobers big dumb wasps

flattened plum sans depth but lots

north of potential slack urge

grasp cookies silky black ear

name a pet whereof it knows

me sure but buddy after

five years bristles at my sight

strangers pocket bacon nonce

prickly grass his barrow busted

who knew between a cubs mitt

and its autumnal polish

me three wafflegate scanner

pulse too slow for radio

high as rural cable dish

loamy froth of circumstance

economy oh ok

blunts face arrow axe or right

plaster hatchet doctorate

suffer liquid liquid heart

souveniring sad mainland

a loop of puppy squeezing

big tears out of its big head

acetone chewies bloody

slippers loves intake drowns out

ecstatic sparking fogtrains

breeze from ouff the buttermilk

under the rose a rubber

tank more limestone shield bearing

europas weighty lemon

horizontals render

unto seizure a marriage

a mix a reader relief

made an american squirm
said we can always take it
back green i mean livery
of my dad clints too a
nickel was it per nato tab
rain but not europe enough
to refresh merciful streams

a rude keeper a claimant
over lahr to gander at
hitlers giftshop dief to jack
a tierack smoked perch soapstoned
shoehorn dewline imprinted
geese prefer parklife rigours
to numismatic limbo

hardingesque fall nutdrop days

onto the eaves like little

burglars brokered kisses

footfall of exclusion coaster

leaf fell bandwidth handover

halicrafter solder sealed

entreaties she is waiting

oh trout of gowanus how

anticipate your needs dredged

too my profligate midden

with less effect oxygen

profit a porcelain

jays wax dollar slice mebbe

layer cake intimate of earth

bye bye my sweet potato

pie an errand a grip look

out for silent correction

nod from an auctioneer six-

ty five ouch my ankle whos

steering not me not me has

left the building genius

sixpence a set said princess
fist duration of pinch to
be determined patterns welt
for waiting textured buff fold
refractive interference
stress and strife the sporting life
as erstering north en point

lacks nickels but freaks techniques
up from drapery your mind
conceals a menaced peasant
orangerie litterbug
barstool maoist facefucker
busy busy fine thanks and your
ass will follow anthrax-breath

harmless pastoral ninny
turn your big brown eyes my way
your birthmark looks like sici-
ly hot wax and honey pour
from you in torrents it
never ends it never stops
crystallised throats of exile

stalinist superferries

bring the landscape closer gray

pudding hills raisined with rain

byzantium without

the rides a squirming marsu-

pial ball endlessly teethes

devouring sex taxation

my dog format screening trees

bushes framing dna

coilers pissy fronds iron

rich beery ruminations

set beetling rocklike snuff

as reading not allowed he

likes you you surprising musk

an ironic improv from

the age of steam shimmering

urbanitys rural re-

ply placating boyars huts

wicker rushed dead parliaments

bearded harvest of inkling

dread williamson curve

high noon for the bourgeoisie

when finally your vaunted

trouble ball staggered across

the plate sweetlet of knowledge

hitherto withheld wafting

on a punk of pitch across

blank arcades of abridgement

equinoctial ache ponies

for instruction the shameless

adoption of powerlessness

as hip fleet intimacies

against totalised cabins

past tree lines of iron whim

through blue crash of four a.m.

baking to the converted

half-cocked on codeine and rice

no pepsi at the laundry

no telly at the inquest

he don't drive carpet burner

led to scuffles led away

wrote on his face like envy

HOMAGE TO QUIZ

dance is what everyone does
mistaking the city for bread
contingency nourished on
pain as ball lightning through
a thickening ozone mist
filtered overpass dust cloaks
anticipations weak mouth

i found a delivery
in my flaw thus sweetened forked
a sutured seams foreclosure
an inning or two blurred
unraveling string-like theory
bowling alley winter wheat
checkered earth from interstate

asterix notwithstanding

footnote your fear permanence

overmasters dans index

the granite mind is split

by commerce through leaves we know

its hockey a cord is two truck-

loads anticipating rim

unnecessary jerky

release favours dilettantes

who by concealment prosper

pocketful of leaves by choice

a hard paperback does not

read itself though by friction

understanding is massaged

estate asunder let no

proposal bearing false heft

countenance signatory

delay upon re-offence

press bestial caretakers

disenfranchise your mood as

if enclosing a thicket

a kid for cause and effect

reproving palisades glum

tableaux of audubon mice

not precisely bearable

a taupe two-set a scratchy

imperial bencher a strap-on

nap from sixty-forth to hoyt

DEDICATED TO YOU BUT YOU WEREN'T LISTENING

rosy gray patina'd sweet

awaits through pocket fuzz its

dry bowl of ham-coloured dawn

blue moon flesh of sandy skate

choky bone sandstone chain glut

bubbled up like verse or cheese

ropy humbug loosed thangs fanks

a fishy syntax supper chips

away an air familiar

giant steps back mr. p.c.

plays out big leash on slacky

collar implied sell-by thwarts

strata counts fool no one try

taking it out of your mouth

clocked glass-blower monologue

with kirk-like contrapuntals

three kinds of misc shit stritch

rounding third or so we heard

a ginger cat of balham

never arrives charm exhaust

fills expenditures damp cave

blank shiny beast of yeoville

aspirative earth heathen

turns over presleys wormy turf

greenworld passing in traintime

walked downwind from the engine

malverns olsonian breasts

worn to a distant pitney

damaged thanet inhalers

reprazent strand frontage

as gruelling conradesque

concealment pebbled with debt

a romanesque resentment

a lean mean archway loafer

pigshaved cornlaw evader

my flat cap forelocks bloody
waving over tea lino
ludo uckers you fuckers
without scale or office
cant climb a marshalsea stack
with sneakers of st. michaels
without knuckles of woolworth

masters if our arms could reach
thumbs could oppose fingering
is half mental fretless slide
from camberwell now to mid-
season loops and replacements
that taste like a deportees
bitter pharmacopia

if a disease skeltonic

not mental fizz nor chronic

defined by lack specific

horror honorific

footdrag ideolectic

nominally terrific

if pseudo-scientific

REASONS WHY I MUMBLE

as though living on handouts

unreproducible crumbs

swept from off planners platters

prayer-rug of faded beach

tans annexations comforts

with educated consent

its assembled alternate

what part of shut the fuck up

responds to bradleys shotgun

pulse of bible paper fuzz

clintonianism

smoked for the taste like nafta

buzz-free worker bee weed

to raise the towering buildings

outside the band present forms

sixtiesish only in that

discontinuity seems

positively valued though

shaded like nodes of greenspace

recorded by a draughtsmens

tremor pedestrianated

an intermittent grid

of metro towns parklike parks

hum with fishes plastic discus

like dishes unseen bug screen

plazas defer arrival

enforcing the center ringed

smudged other dogs feeling off

self-regulating cash crop

pays for itself pays itself

unbruiseable peach content

settles during sleepovers

but how otherwise bear their bad

pink baby faces rapt with

glee staring staring at me

oh shit here it comes again

the unformed armys star system

hierarchic quasar plaid

volcanic but bespoke

imaginary poverty

with real rags pornographic

transparency compulsory

marking up the emulsion

maintaining tone a tan kind of coat

gnomically needy waving

like that purple rothko cloud

reproduced from last night

identical conditions

except the pears have fallen

a barney to the great wen

a bargeman thinks with inspots

a passing pear polisher

forced to draw a diagram

bout the way he feels leth-

ridge to bonneville natchez to mo-

bile ladysmith to duncan

random traffic has different

problems turning space

over to circulation

so-called factual research

but not near not really car

or some similar machine

the system of another

the pear tree wont last we'll see

if will is stronger than white

glue or the limewash mellors

favors the gift of coffee

is an act of love the bench

tells time like all things sunny

twice a day or thereabouts

core city overall cluster

steel tables bent under weight of snow

hierarchies of traffic

backed off the main road we wait

for services nurturing

beefs and bouquets tilley caps

tilted against the icy fog

three families acre outwards

decompacting the trees

thinning a feeling of having

arrived at a pedestrian deck

an era of good feelings

green striped caterpillars through

the fennel because you said so

a place of identity

or pastoral mind silage

we played our musty part signed

off on the waterfronts flags

the holiday camps where bach

wakes you up for a headcount

metallica tucks you in

snake eyes when two sevens clash

green roofs of one another

systematic and humane

passing over at a great height

who can tell where it begins

park or yard or factory

the lights of the deltaport

House Is a Feeling

for Daphne

House is a feeling.

A thing
      to which other things are added.

      120 beats per minute give or take —

A point where concrete foundations

      gravel off into fields, lift
          over tracks
      hedges, trellis, white

shutters, trails off hung window limp
yellow lace like smoke, half-basement's

      asbestos green grid upturned
flaking chainlink submerged in

deadly unreachable blackberry. Pipe tobacco
smell of new hay, futz

      of weekday stretchers
      double income

rural types, *rentiers,*
pensionnaires
lacking only ruffles

blinkered petting
as if to
rub up against it
were sufficient —

a llama peering through
the towering fennel
emits a hard sharp buzz
over its hinged lower teeth
but cannot otherwise
disguise its interest

A certain hitch
a flatted fifth
and then it's as if
you're singing:

Mr. Fingers
bangs a skillet
against a retaining wall
and they are all retaining walls,

airlessly pressing
his hard thumb
on my reddened thorax —

south of that you
might as well float away
if transfer you seek,
transfusion
like steam off a workshop roof

A long mixed block of Milton
flat a little shiny, overhung
granite cladded, blasted smooth
but then laterally
scored and scratched
as if by cats,
grain elevator, wild garden
overspill, holly welt,
shredded bales of wire
padlocked lumberyard —
The reign of
piety and iron
concluded:

a flattened fork (he argues)
a business card from a Honda dealer (speaks)
a broad bright yellow leaf (a map)
creased where the tide broke (foxed)
a sedimentary reversal

Divided it and then
divided it again
a rolling snare
a drop
divided kick, then split
divide it again
and then oh up
from the engine room
from the inside
from the outside

Oh monumentalising beam!
Refulgent 303!
On waves and waves of filtered pink
carpet this afternoon!

By the South Gate
        the north advances
dollar-store early birds prop
        no frontage no street corner no size
surf's up cabinets of
        yellowish dust
they seen it was only
        in the space it took
Ives to pan the cortège
        with an archival flicker:

a ragged line that ran across the windowsill
red Topaz umbrella lowering
palm leaves with a damp cloth
everything south of the fold
muffled unanswered
muted stanchion
resurfaced spongiform roadway
gives way to a park
about eighteen foot square
                all gate

a parting gift
                from a beloved creditor
                with an unsurprisable mind;

a client state
                addressed from a thinking cloud

reversals gleam
like dew on an unmown lawn

speech or its opposite
flutters the blinds
at the moment of sleep —

The Voice of Kathy Sledge

'The green morocco binding of the spring,
emblazoned with blue stamping.'
— JAMES SCHUYLER

the voice of kathy sledge —
stevie's another star, the
long melismatic fade now
as in '79 once again most
of the song —
echoes outward faintly
through the window over
the blue railing to
the grey snow, as if
my taste had somehow
saved me
from the question of
imaginary shutters and
then of making sure
the actual door is properly shut
which it often isn't, or why
the sifto consumer grade road salt
glimmering faintly, pearly,
bounces off the clouds off
the sweet potato water orange
light from town, and
on the stairs seems
to draw from the frozen wood
a thin layer of sap
slick as five-in-one
destabilising the
thin grit underfoot —
within shotgun
outside of porchlight

seventeen versions
of la buena vida —
forms fill themselves in
with poignant dependability
shapes you like I like
the ones with acoustic guitars
the ones that make you cry
a page from locke
ground into oil,
rolled on the buttery
leaves of the 39 articles, dipped
in formaldeheyde
and left to dry
a blunt as big as a badger
a vancouver special with
obverse lions
rampant meringue
treetop tea-rose pillar
rinsed-out bungalow
roofs reflect
the oxidised light above
your spindly widow's walk
the space in the air
it occupied
jupiter, comfy
on the lip of a blue hill
but once again
the twinkling attention
of the lights below
chills the remix, a cat
sets off a motion sensor
and an operating theatre
appears beneath
an infant's basketball hoop
a mode of deliverance
once entered into

even the crabgrass
asserts in dimpled relief
its ancient encroachment —
all down the line
by invective transfer
the means by which
this or that domain is secured
woodgrain panelled rv habitat
oddly sloping wide
sidewalk but you trip
carport, or south of there
shed, or out here
dogbark instead of shotgun
berkeley instead of locke

A Letter From Hammertown to East Vancouver and the East Village

dear K. —

I'm planning ahead
    for the first time —

for soon it will be spring
    and then it will be the grid of appearance

upon which spring can be laid.
    That is, what is from the ground up
        becoming

will be from the æther
    managed —
        the lawns will fade to unfenced ochre,

back onto alleys, roughly narrow paved
    (the width of an Austin

from the administration of Macmillan)
    the poignant sheds will sprawl and lean

another season
    for no reason.

But all of this, though hardly molecular,
    — if squinted at through eyes oracular —

betrays conclusions scarcely singular:
    the scale is still a cap full of cabbage

resting on a bag of flesh
    pulled along by a little red wagon —

what eventually emerges
        from dirty stubby fingers toes
                beggars description

but is no secret, either.
        a deer trail,
                then a dog trail,
                        then Pete's trail,

then my trail. Sherpa Tenzing sits puffing
        on the roof of the world —

his belief in process absorbed
        by the throbbing worm

that mutters and sweats
        at the mucky heart
                of being . . .

Thus engaged,
        rhetoric becomes prosthesis,

staggers down the parade route
        of a strange city
                within a giant face of plaster —

but speak!
                it does not.

Another grotesquerie
        affirming
                the shapeliness of all things — likewise

the saturate flowers, the seepage
        suspect, the coffee grounds
                idling in the tray — such that

progressive collapse seems itself a tender unfolding,
    a rose within a bible drying,
        a whiff of distant evening cooking

The winter twilight's pall of woodsmoke
    drifts and softens

even as it sears and conceals —
    just as the low millennial fog of Hammertown
        cloaks the shuttered factories, dog-ridden lots and

oil-dappled pavements
    in the wispy raiments
        of authenticity . . .

I stirred the pondwater
    with a little stick, watched
        duckweed swirl

as though beneath
    February's late ice, while
        through the bright fractal enclosures

of the alder grove
    flickers flicked, towhees wheeled
        tanagers managed —

I'm lining things up
    all in a little row
        so that the real image of spring

and the mental image of spring
    can be made to somehow agree —

the new incorporated self
    erects a kind of recording scrim, on which

the successive domed apprehensions
    of the April sky, the

broiling surface tension of Dodd Narrows, etc.
    can be decelerated and examined —

a field guide to fields, a boy's book of burls,
the unexamined yard, fern monochrome attribution,
dull days in the eastern capitals . . .

    the index: the big one

these wet streets, your hands
    plunged into the warm dirt, the exhaust fans
        of the endless orange tunnel that lies between us,

what of them?
    I try to think of you
        and can bring to mind
            only the great parabolic bridges
        in whose shadow you live, fist-sized rivets
            of red iron, buoying above
        the molten stream of thought

into which
    each day you are thrown!

As the day grows clear and cold
    the mind grows hazy, the wind-indicating
        woodpecker hesitates
    and reverses; the earth, like a little
        boat on a calm day
    pitches and rolls, a metal stylus

on a resonating film
    of charged oil

Eight Views of Ornamental Avenue

1.

Sad Uncle Chimp
caught looking
worse!

Caught weeping!

Tears soak the flocking
of your old retainer's
livery, pearl
and fall
to the floor.

An Old Master
with aquavit breath
might have added
a ruby or gold chain
to your dowry,
suggested in the shading
of the overturned punchbowl
a symbolic cat
bolt upright
in the corner,
a fragment of ham
lodged in your goatee —
but the masque has ended
the picture's varnished,
the pavilion's blue stripes
mended and folded,
buckets of icemelt
poured out on the lawn.

2.

The drunken commodore,
whose only weekend chore
had been to choose between
the white and yellow moons
wuffles awake inside his cap
at the back of the boathouse,
outside and on the windows beads
the kind of Celtic mist
birds like, also
soaking it up
the furry flowers
under the lawnmower's blade.

The dandelions
already
white-headed ghosts.

He'd dreamt
the seasons and conversations
had mulched themselves
and that from their base
a clear sweet liquid
had been extracted.

3.

The Boiled Owl
shudders in his shawl
but otherwise don't
move at all.
Vast eyes popped open

five seconds since
but here's hopin'
his wince-inducing
dog and pony act
can just this once
dangle and not trickle,
allowing for a slow
Gordo chiaroscuro
style fade
on our part, up and
out and back
back back, cause
not even a lickle
of his ruffled accusations
and spattered cravats
are where it's at.

The breezes in the treetops would say:
please put your notebook away.

The birds in the hedges would add:
he's not your dad.

4.

In Maida Vale
did Delia Derbyshire
string down the hallway
a 40-foot loop
of iron oxide
stuck with rice and salt
to make a sound
that would be sellotaped
to another sound

ten thousand times
to assemble an anthem
for the Queen of Cypress.

The charge that held
the cellophane cigarette wrapper
against her waving fingers
contained a perfect arpeggio
she knew, lacking
only the means
to coax itself from the æther
through the oscilliscope's
shaded green grid,
magnet and foil
its ascending call
along the tiles,
tobacco curtains
the thick September air
over the North Circular.

5.

We're nine or ten
minutes in
the rhythm section
blooming upward
from the bass
has filled the stereo field:

Fela Kuti takes
a few stabs in that
Sun Ra meets Sly Stone
Fender Rhodes mode
that defers and defers

with blithe complexity,
all in the matter
of delaying
the reason we put the record
on in the first place,
that moment when the horns
come in and everything goes
   BIG and WIDE
the gruff-edged baritones
mark even more time
with a series
of barks and squacks
and then boom,
mauve curtain descending:

it is at this point
that DJ Theo Parrish
drops the bass completely out
concentrating the massed overtones
of Africa '70
into a shimmering
yellow blur against
the walls of a thin jar

an unknown song
from a transistor
hung from the rear-view
of a car passing
over the bridge
under which you sit
hands pressed
against your ears.

6.

There's only one explosion
and it's about one hour
and three minutes into the movie.

   William Daniels
on a yacht
jumpy in his admiral outfit
and with good reason
it turns out.

Blunted by
three decades
of quotation — the yacht
now in the distance,
soundless poof,
in for a grainy closeup
on the now roaring flames —
it's easy to forget
how much more decisively
Pakula's modest
interruption of the horizon
announced the imperium's
deliberate reach —
its ultimately calm approach —
than the petulant shotgun of Hopper
or the café apocalypse
of Antonioni —

a blink in broad daylight
before a bitter disposition

over which your paintings layer
the cops outside

in full pre-riot mode, the
victorious honking
restrained even on Robson —
the particulate drift
of the spectators
moving around inside.

7.

If I were a bell
I'd keep coming back,
because it's different
every time. This kind
of bumpy ride
is a very new thing —
the clarity of the edits,
pennants snapping you
to mild attention,
     a surge
     of pigeons
     glimmering silver and cocoa
     above the rooftops
     like anti-radar foil
     as you stumble outside
     montage —

I'll play it
and tell you
what it is
later

(in a voice
not the dry rasp
it will become) —

Look — you,
sitting there
regarding the flickering dials
of the walnut soundboard
before you
like numbers on a ticker,
box cutter through your belt —

you see that pink granite tomb
relecting so majestically
this late afternoon?

Well they're keeping it
for me.

So don't phase out
mistaking the eyelash kiss
for disdain, the
hard masks and
turning away
for lack of interest, we
(and I mean me)
need your skill
more than your fear.

Once, our work
farmed out, cut
by talented strangers
from bolts of like cloth
could get by
        without your special sauce,
        songs falling like fruit
        in a common orchard,
        a play was a machine
        that laughed.

Everything was hung
with little silver chimes,
or so it seemed, volleyballs
and little carts
rolled gently downhill,
creosote and warm hay
where they stopped.

When you look up
(and you will)
the annihilating blue fog
at your feet
will have given way
to the warm light
of a provisional regard —

and by this kind
of gentle tuning
will you know me.

8.

Little by little
the wind erodes our *oeuvres*
till nothing is left
but a golden bee
holding up a tapestry,

lattices through which
content can
occasionally be glimpsed
receding in tabbyish twilight.

From the tightening
Crown Royal bag
of the sky
a tea-stained document
is produced, marked
here, here and
here

Don't let it fool you.
No warrant holders scribble
or waxen pawprint
will evict us from this
acreage and entail,
even as little by little
the margins are trimmed and
the marshes are drained.

No chit
will evict me
from this yeomanry.

Journey to the West

1.

The accordionist's black-key stabs cause the humid air to ripple in a pulse of pink mist above the dancer's heads. The clank of the pocket-sized tractor and grader spreading dirt over the thickly aldered meadow over the old mine entrance, through which the scabs were chased by anarcho-syndicalist Finns just one step ahead of the King's army. Covering the still-abundant mine tailings with loamy topsoil continues that work of Empire, I guess. The mild threat behind the neighbour's lawn enquiry that Dorn points out. Not a recipe for a hockey riot, surely. More the agreeable filibuster of a cherished companion animal nosing against the lintel.

2.

The pivot wobbles. Lying there about the level of Ozu's camera your head pans slowly left, then right, as if brushing its gaze against the yellow cakes of early afternoon light. Upturned briar carousel with two little drawers, rusty rings of boullion. The clock's ticking for those young maples almost brushing the power line. Occupation is such an ugly word. Settling is what dust does best, and if they can't be relied upon to unseal their bids, why not just open up the jails? Pioneers of quietude will trade their cudgels and wooden shoes for brooms and sandals.

3.

From the frog around his waist he drew a small hatchet or claw hammer to hit those chords of Ur. Under the gentle demand of Wooley's soft sable the cuneiform floats into legibility. The Phantom Melody. The part of Dvorak's Sonata for Wind that they got Bali H'ai from.

Odd fragments of rolling stock that pass through include the late seventies schoolbus yellow truck adapted for rail travel and maintenance and the guys that do that might as well be in a sandbox they're so happy. By the Blue Hawaiian Shore — tone picture. Laughter throughout his memoirs written as har har har. Not since they switched back but for a while they got rid of the weeds at the side of the track not by cutting them (as they do now) or by poisoning them (which they did for a couple of years to great uproar) but by steaming them to death with a kind of mobile kettle sporting a set of insect leg attachments that allowed themselves to be lowered, a dozen spouts on each leg firing in a big wet cloud, to within inches of the ground. Three Fanciful Sketches. Bleached white as if the chlorophyll had simply evaporated.

4.

Not really a holler so much as a bowl, into which sounds enter or leave only with difficulty. The peacocks up the street, the parakeet up the other street, the low rumble of Rail America, whose patriotically festooned cars once hauled freight daily through the muttering Commonwealth to the Port Alberni sawmill, gone now but for the once a week legal requirement that all eight cars ceremonially replicate the old route. The maintenance of a footpath, in common law. One of those placed where the Empire, appearing to recede, re-advances as a ghost.

5.

Three soldiers trapped behind enemy lines when *Full Metal Jacket* left town, chasing Captain America with a bamboo camera. The third bumble-bee-sized spring fly in as many quarter hours means it's time to put the screen in, which since I took it down and dusted it last October has mysteriously gotten dusty again; too fucking bad. Also I'd had to keep the blinds down so as not to attract into the house the sparrows nesting in the neighbour's big walnut just outside my window, who treat every local portal as a real estate opportunity, later the dumb post-nestlings who won't know where they are. The grid of the screen more apparent to them I think. They can fly up to the window all they want.

Morse's Code

for Lee Ann & Tony
'did you expect southern butter?'

1.

You have no memory of it,
but something —
the way maybe
Sam Waterston's coat
drapes across his arm
as he quickly runs
up the courthouse steps —
tells you it's a repeat,
or the feeling through
your whole body
outward from the hand and
up from the rebar,
striking adamantine
sparks across fillings,
flaking paper leaves,
knocking pebbles
grounders four feet
into Ladysmith harbour
off Transfer Beach
the satisfying plonk
of the heavy flat pebble
dropping deep,
crack of driftwood bat,
elicits from Liam
(for whom speech then
    at best
a lightly regarded register)
a momentary keening

then a sustained
intake of breath,
commencing as if
to a smoke-filled
brocaded armour room
an impromptu address:
a butter knife
taps a water glass,
rhetorical quietus
crosses his face like a cloud —
phylogenetic like the Method
then gone like a cool breeze.

Or it could be the way
the pale pink petals
of the asterish
catnip flowers
(dislodged by
extirpated bees,
also pale, dusty,
greenish yellow
faintly striped)
arrange themselves
on the blue stained porch
with studied thitherness,
slightness edging
manipulation, endearing
scatter, chaotic
like a certain kind
of good day, supine
like Goethe
on the downy spine
of the continental divide;
with a dark card
and some thin glue
you prepare to make

a record, voices
from below and above
press the soft walls
of the amniotic ether
no more roughly
than do the receding
velvety peaks
of the old America,
the mound America.

2.

An odd feeling of floating
toes dragging heavenward
occupies the near-silence
left by the generator's
abrupt and shuddering shutdown,
various birds and dogs
shouting over it all along
amp down gratefully
if not gracefully,
crimped green pipes
secured with collars rest
on fresh drifts of topsoil
until the sun
takes everything out of the picture.

Genre completes it later —
a grey scale out of Blakey
over an Ottoman blue sky,
lozenged skidmarks
        in ochre ditchspace,
icebarrel transcription discus
nonchantly half-boomeranging

over earnest lego capitals,
coming to rest beside a toy ball
whose decorative stars have been
eroded by saliva.

As formerly in Davenport
similarly excavated, similarly
    licked
they took their gin
with coloured bulbs
in clouds of Kolnisch wasser
and the victrola-horned astringencies
of Mr. Albert Ketelby's bells
to assert half-nauseated
synesthestic drift as appropriate
response to either
their dad's horehound-smelling
Barbasol babbitry
or the post-Wilsonian
inward turn, so did we dwell

    "in a monastery garden"

hanging the notes like apples on a tree

(our Whitman via *Delius*,
    for fuck's sake)

so through the dark trellises of Harewood
    did we array against
the hegemony of Social Credit
and the pirate mayor
the tattooed maxims of Philip Whalen
    and the heaving crystallographies
of Wanda Landowska:
    it was as if

her harpsichord
had by some device
imprinted itself
on the heavy old vinyl,
so worn a web of little scratches
was visible in the careening
ribbon of light that straddled
the picture frame's pale curved limit,
translucent carriages bursting
mysterious barricades,
her paws as soft as Scottish weather
floating in scare quotes
above the podium
all we could see
from where we sat.